D0571663

Mama Used to Say

WIT & WISDOM
↤ *from the* ↦
HEART & SOUL

Hannibal B. Johnson

© 2003 by Hannibal B. Johnson

First printing 2003. Third printing 2013.

Published in the United States by:

Hannibal B. Johnson, Esq.

AUTHOR, ATTORNEY & CONSULTANT

121 North Greenwood Avenue, Suite G

Tulsa, Oklahoma 74120

www.hannibalbjohnson.com

LIBRARY OF CONGRESS CATALOG-IN-PUBLICATION DATA

Johnson, Hannibal
Mama used to say : wit & wisdom from the heart & soul / Hannibal B. Johnson
    p. cm.
ISBN 1-930709-46-3 (alk. paper)
    1. Johnson, Hannibal B.–Childhood and youth. 2. Johnson family. 3. AfricanAmericans–Arkansas–Biography. 4. African American mothers–Arkansas–Biography. 5. Arkansas–Biography. 6. African American mothers–Quotations. 7. Conduct of life–Quotations, maxims, etc. 8. Social values–United States–Quotations, maxims, etc. 9. Meditations. 10. African Americans–Arkansas–Social conditions–20th century. I. Title.
F415.3.J64A3 2003
158.1–dc22

                                                        2003056697

Printed in the United States

COVER AND BOOK DESIGN: Carl Brune

Table of Contents

Forword   V

Acknowledgements   VII

I.   LIFE & LIVING   1

II.   FAMILY & RELATIONSHIPS   5

III.   RIGHT & WRONG   11

IV.   MONEY & WORK   17

V.   TIME   21

VI.   SUCCESS & FAILURE   25

VII.   RACE   29

VIII.   RELIGION   33

IX.   LOVE   37

X.   RESPECT   41

XI.   EDUCATION   45

XII.   INTEGRITY   49

XIII.   CITIZENSHIP   53

XIV.   PERSEVERANCE   57

XV.   HONESTY   61

XVI.   HUMILITY   65

XVII.   GRACE   69

XVIII.   COMPASSION   73

XIX.   OPPORTUNITY   77

XX.   HOPE   81

Epilogue   85

PROLOGUE

I owe much of my modest success to the thoughtful guidance and wise counsel of my mother. I offer this book in partial repayment of a tremendous debt of gratitude.

Mama Used To Say contains a smattering of the pearls of wisdom and gems of wit that I learned from my mother. I am by no means unique. Mothers around the world lovingly pass along to their children timeless expressions, sage advice, and bedrock values.

The precious jewels shared within may resurrect fond memories, elicit a joyous smile, or evoke a bittersweet tear. Whether growing up or growing old, searching one's soul or searching for one's soul mate, moving up the corporate ladder or moving out of the line of fire, *Mama Used To Say* contains something especially for you.

This tribute features a sampling of Mama's remarkable lessons, through precept and example, on navigating the ebb and flow of life's ever-shifting waters. I offer these simple yet profound truths to you with the same cheerfulness and love with which I received them from Mama. May the pages that follow stimulate your mind, warm your heart, and soothe your soul.

ACKNOWLEDGEMENTS

*T*hanks to the following individuals for their contributions to this work: First and foremost, my mother, Bernice West Johnson; my father, Frank Johnson; my siblings, Joan Johnson Good, Brenda Johnson Portis, David Johnson, Magnus Johnson, and Frank Johnson III; my aunt, Doris West Wilson; Cheryl Brown; and Nancy Day. I offer a special note of gratitude to my dear friend, Judith A. Colbert, Esq., who provided some of the initial inspiration for this project.

I

LIFE & LIVING

*Life has meaning only if one barters it day by day for some-
thing other than itself.* ~ Saint-Exupéry (1948)

My older brother, Magnus, a fiercely determined child,
simply refused to give up. That unflinching determination sometimes resulted in unanticipated, unwelcome
consequences.

As children in rural Ar-
kansas, we saw a good deal
of the great outdoors. That,
of course, meant extensive
exposure to garden variety
"critters." Magnus, being a
bright and curious kid, relished the opportunity to get
out and about and commune
with nature. At eight years
old, he learned an unmistakable lesson: Nature's bountiful
rewards come with varying
degrees of risk.

On the day in question, a
sunny, sultry, summer after-
noon, we frolicked innocently in the vast expanse of our
rustic backyard. A dizzying array of sights and smells
awaited. Succulent purple grapes swelled in Dad's mini-
vineyard just steps from our front door. Yellowish-orange
persimmons dangled from a tree abutting the house. Red-
olent honeysuckle collided with pungent wild onions as
the competing smells wafted through the molasses-thick
air.

1

Without warning, an obviously irritated honeybee spotted Magnus, took aim, and descended full bore on its target. The bee scored a direct hit. Showing no mercy, it injected its complex, barbed stinger, then took flight. The detached stinger, now embedded in Magnus' skin, pumped a steady stream of potent venom into his small body.

Magnus, with lightning speed, snatched the offending bee from mid-air, clinched the whirring pest in his diminutive, nimble hand, and squeezed the tiny, winged assailant with all his might. Riled and sensing grave peril, the bug put up a do-or-die defensive struggle.

Magnus screamed and hollered as he writhed in pain. Mama, rushing to the rescue, tried in vain to get him to release the bee. He stubbornly refused. Unwavering, and with the vise-like crush of his firmly clutched fist, he imposed capital punishment. Magnus reigned supreme.

Apparently, Mama and Dad aptly named their fourth child: Magnus Conquest Johnson. Magnus means "great" in Latin. Conquest speaks for itself.

Magnus remained resolute and defiant, even in the face of acute pain. The experience left a lifelong impression. With Mama's guidance, Magnus discovered that sometimes attending to the victim takes precedence over punishing the victimizer. Often after a sting or a setback, self-examination becomes the top priority. Like Mama says, be flexible while remaining committed.

Mama's Pearls

- *Feed your enemies with a long-handled spoon.*

- *Can't and won't are cousins —can't is the son of never-try and won't is the son of woe.*

- *You've got a tough row to hoe.*

- *The first hen that cackles is the hen that laid the egg.*

- *Words are like toothpaste— once you get them out, there's no putting them back in.*

MEDITATION

Life is worth living—a simple, yet profound, message. Amazingly, far too few of us behave that way. We amble through life moaning and groaning, focused intently on all that goes wrong instead of all that goes right. We count our burdens instead of our blessings. Life's bumps and bruises usually heal, and we grow stronger.

Scaling life's peaks can be sweet. Reaching those summits becomes even sweeter when we recall the valleys we passed through on the way up.

FIRST THINGS FIRST: Count your blessings—literally. List some of the many things for which you can be thankful. List any obstacles you overcame—and how you managed to overcome them—in order to realize the positives in your life.

3

II

FAMILY & RELATIONSHIPS

There is no hope of joy except in human relations.

~ SAINT-EXUPÉRY (1942)

My eldest sister, Joan—"Jo," for short—gives truth to the adage, "The acorn doesn't fall far from the tree." She embodies equal parts of the personas of Mama and Dad.

Mama exudes compassion. She cares how others feel. Dad radiates tenacity. He stakes out a position, and rarely retreats from it. Jo inherited Mama's heart and Dad's will. Tragedy forged a bittersweet alliance between those two traits.

My oldest brother, David—"Dave"—died of terminal cancer in 1988. Family and relationships undergirded his journey from diagnosis to death.

In 1984, Dave's dentist discovered a small, painless growth near one of his lower molars. Subsequent examinations by doctors led to a grim finding: cancer of the salivary glands. Ironically, Dave lived just a couple of miles from the renowned M.D. Anderson Cancer Center in Houston, Texas, one of the country's foremost cancer treatment facilities.

Knowing that radical surgery loomed on the horizon, Dave called Mama in Fort Smith, Arkansas to break the news. His carefully crafted message to Mama reflected his ever-present concern for her feelings and overall well-being.

Dave always maintained a close relationship with Mama, talking with her regularly by phone and visiting at least twice a year. He admired her dedication to the family—her willingness to do whatever the circumstances demanded. Whenever Dave's schedule required him to work through Christmas, Mama would bake, then carefully wrap, one of his favorites—an applesauce cake—and mail it to him. Time and time again, the cake arrived fresh, nary a crumb out of place. Grateful for all the things that Mama did, Dave especially relished Mother's Day. He unfailingly showered her with gifts of gold jewelry or precious stones—indulgences she would not likely purchase for herself.

During this particularly difficult call, Dave calmly explained the situation. He reassured Mama that he would face this new challenge one day at a time and continue to make the best of his life. He asked that she not worry, noting that he would be in the hands of the best cancer treatment center in the nation.

Next, Dave called my sister, Brenda, in Northern California. He reviewed the conversation with Mama, then said, "Stay strong. We have things to do." Without pause, he launched into his meticulously detailed plan of action. He asked Brenda to come to Houston a few days prior to the surgery to assist with the admissions process and secure an apartment across the street from M.D. Anderson for family members. He requested that she do research on cancer of the salivary glands at The University of Texas Medical Library. "You're the nurse," he said, "so I want you here to help me through the medical part." Dave made one more request: "When you come to Houston, bring your nice business suits, heels, and hats—plenty of hats. I want you to make an impression on the folks here at M.D. Anderson." Finally, he noted that he planned to ask Jo to stay with him following his discharge.

Dave called me in advance of the surgery. He disclosed

his plan, including his careful orchestration of a family support network. Detecting my shock at the news, and perhaps sensing my feeling of utter impotence, he assured me that everything would be fine. "The best thing you can do," he noted, "is to keep on doing what you're doing." A third-year law student at Harvard at the time, I was just weeks from graduation.

The moment of truth arrived. In 1984, Dave underwent radical oral surgery and radiation treatment. Brenda, Jo, my brother, Magnus, and Mama cared for him in Houston during his post-operation recuperative period. I use the phrase "cared for" guardedly. Dave, strong, intelligent, and quick-witted, cherished his independence. His fierce pride would allow only so much outside intervention, even from inside the family. Still, he valued family enormously. He kept constantly in touch with all of us by way of personal visits, telephone calls, and correspondence. With family support, Dave made it through his initial ordeal.

When his cancer recurred in 1988, Dave withheld the true gravity of his illness for as long as he could. Intuitively, Jo suspected a marked deterioration in Dave's health, so she flew to Houston from Fort Smith.

In Houston, she discovered a weak and rapidly diminishing Dave. Despite his best pretenses, Dave could not shroud his fragility and fatigue from the watchful eyes of his big sister. Jo sensed the worst.

Not long after that visit, Jo and her husband, Leo, decided to move Dave from Houston to their home in Fort Smith. Jo wanted Dave to be as comfortable, worry-free, and well cared for as possible. She knew that being surrounded by family and friends would lift his spirits. Moreover, his presence would reassure family and friends that his needs—physical, emotional, and spiritual—were being met. My brother, Frank, flew to Houston to help with the move and to drive Dave's prized black and gold Pontiac Trans Am back to Fort Smith.

Dave knew that the trip from Houston to Fort Smith would be his last. By now gaunt and debilitated, Dave nonetheless refused to let Frank drive his car out of Houston. "I drove myself into this city, and I'll drive myself out," he bellowed. Once outside the Houston city limits, pained pride and steely determination gave way to harsh reality. Exhausted, Dave surrendered the wheel to Frank.

In Fort Smith, Dave declined physically, but remained mentally sharp. His final day began normally. Mama and Dad came over to stay with him while Jo went to work. About midmorning, Dave asked Mama to call Jo. Mama gently reminded him that Jo would be home for lunch in about thirty minutes. Not satisfied, Dave insisted that Mama call Jo home immediately. Mama called Jo at the office. Jo made her way home. Her arrival freed Dave to head home as well.

Dave knew that his time had come—that he would take his last breath that day. He wanted Jo there to take charge of the situation and to comfort Mama and Dad. His final act—leaving everything in Jo's capable hands—served as an incredible acknowledgement of her boundless devotion, and doubled as a tribute to family. Family really does matter. And—the acorn really does not fall far from the tree.

Mama's Pearls

- *A long life may not be good enough, but a good life is long enough.*
- *Blood is thicker than water.*
- *Weight is what broke the wagon.*

MEDITATION

The bonds of kinship and affinity form the ties that bind. Yet no family is perfect; no relationship flawless. We have much to learn from the experiences of those who came before us. We can build on their triumphs and learn from their mistakes.

Family and relationships remind us that each of us is a part of something larger than ourselves. That sense of belonging, of loving and being loved, makes us human. When we become self-important and self-absorbed, we need a loved one with the courage to step in and remind us that the center of the universe lies elsewhere.

FIRST THINGS FIRST: Think about all the relationships that are important to you, including family relationships. List them. For each relationship you identified, list at least three things that you commit to do that will nurture and enhance it.

III

RIGHT & WRONG

To do a great right, do a little wrong.

~ WILLIAM SHAKESPEARE (1596-97)

In 1962, the Johnson family moved from Coal Hill, Arkansas to that state's second largest city, Fort Smith. My sister, Brenda, enrolled as a fifteen-year-old senior for her first and final year at Fort Smith's segregated, all-Black, Lincoln High School.

The existence of school segregation in Fort Smith came as no surprise. In tiny Coal Hill, Brenda and my other school-aged siblings routinely boarded a bus—not a school bus, but a regular commercial bus—on school days. They bypassed several White schools en route to the downtown bus station in neighboring Clarksville, a larger town. They walked from the downtown bus station to the town's "Colored" school.

Cramped quarters, too few teachers, and the absence of a library hobbled the school. Moreover, what few books the school managed to acquire came mainly from its teachers' personal collections or as hand-me-downs from the neighboring White schools. Despite these hardships, "Colored" children learned.

The slow pace of progress in rural Arkansas notwithstanding, Blacks in Fort Smith began to chip away at the stone walls of segregation. Weary of second-class citizenship, they embraced the burgeoning civil rights movement. My parents joined the ranks of those freedom fighters. Almost immediately, Mama and Dad signed up with

11

the Fort Smith chapter of the National Association for the Advancement of Colored People, the NAACP. Throughout the nation, the NAACP pressed for racial equality and launched a barrage of legal challenges to pry open the doors to educational opportunity for Blacks.

Dr. Harry P. McDonald, the sole Black physician in Fort Smith, served as NAACP President. He practiced extensively at St. Edward Hospital, and formed a bond with the Sisters of Mercy, operators of the hospital and St. Edward School of Nursing.

Dr. McDonald worked quietly, diplomatically, and methodically with two of the Sisters, the director of nursing and the hospital administrator, to chip away at the bulwark of segregation surrounding St. Edward School of Nursing. He handpicked two Black girls whom he knew could meet or exceed all entry requirements, withstand the enormous pressures associated with acting as change agents, and successfully complete the prescribed course of study. Brenda, who excelled in school, saw opportunity in every challenge, and displayed a passion for the medical profession, made Dr. McDonald's short list. He needed Mama and Dad to bless the mission.

True to form, Brenda anxiously accepted the role of barrier-breaker. Given her earnestness and eagerness, Mama and Dad required little convincing. They knew that she measured up to the task. They spoke with the Sisters, successfully reassuring them that their daughter, though young, matched the other entering students both intellectually and by any measure of maturity.

Mama and Dad believed in Brenda. With equal vigor, they believed in the rightness of their cause. Segregation was simply wrong. With the wholehearted support of Mama and Dad, Brenda entered St. Edward School of Nursing during the summer of 1963.

The Sisters and the other nursing students generally supported integration. Warm, welcoming, and supportive, they helped transform a potentially volatile situation into a relatively comfortable one. Nonetheless, Brenda faced her share of challenges, great and small.

Early on, the Sisters paired her with her first patient, a middle-aged White woman. One evening, the woman engaged Brenda in some polite banter. She asked sheepishly, "What nationality are you, honey?" Brenda replied, courteously, "Negro." "Negro!" the woman exclaimed. "No, don't say that, dear," she continued. "You should tell people you're anything *but* a Negro," she screeched.

The woman, seeing this fair-skinned, "passable" girl, no doubt wondered why anyone would *choose* to self-classify as a "Negro." She figured that Brenda could "pass" for a member of some other racial or ethnic group, and should take full advantage of the ambiguity surrounding her racial identity.

Brenda, bristling at the suggestion and eager to set the record straight, retorted, "Yes, I'm a Negro and proud of it. Why would I want to deny who I am?" Flustered, the woman attempted to explain, "I just thought it would be easier for you, dear." The subject never resurfaced.

Somewhat later, Brenda and her classmates prepared to attend a much-anticipated weekend dance. Excited about this break from their regimented schedule, the girls of St. Edward anxiously shed their workaday wardrobes for more glamorous attire. They anticipated meeting interesting, eligible bachelors at the soiree. As it turned out, the guys at the dance—all of them soldiers; all of them White—came from a nearby military base, Fort Chaffee. Brenda, determined to make the most of this rare social gathering, mingled, chatted, and danced the night away, scarcely aware of violating the firmly ensconced "race mixing" taboo.

The next week, a young man from the dance came calling. The gentleman, handsome, well-mannered, and well-spoken, approached the dormitory housemother.

"I'm here to see Miss Brenda Johnson," he explained. An awkward silence followed. Finally, stunned and stone-faced, the housemother replied, "Why, don't you know she's *Colored*?" Undaunted and undeterred, the soldier suitor responded ever so politely, "Yes, ma'am, I do. Please call her for me." The housemother, a product of her times, reluctantly acquiesced, momentarily suspending her deeply ingrained view that proper White boys simply do not show romantic interest in Colored girls.

Despite such subtle (and sometimes not so subtle) slights, in June of 1966 nineteen-year-old Brenda became the first Black graduate of St. Edward School of Nursing. She successfully completed her examinations and received her license as a registered nurse.

Doing the right thing always entails costs. Often, we need a courageous pioneer to blaze the trail to our future. Like Mama says, anything worth having is worth paying for. Today, Brenda's portrait adorns the halls of St. Edward Mercy Medical Center, a sprawling medical complex in Fort Smith.

Mama's Pearls

~✖ *You can always find an empty seat on a bus going in the wrong direction.*

~✖ *Two wrongs don't make* **one** *right.*

~✖ *An eye for an eye leaves everybody blind.*

~✖ *If you look for trouble, you'll find it.*

MEDITATION

Cultivating a proper sense of right and wrong in a child—providing him or her with a "moral compass"—poses enormous challenges. Yet, few gifts from adult to child offer greater rewards.

Children need clarity. They crave certainty. They deserve guidance. Admittedly, much in our world often seems an unsettling shade of gray. But by instilling a sense of morality in our children, we equip them with the tools necessary to sort through much of the ambiguity.

FIRST THINGS FIRST: Take some time to reflect on your own "moral compass." List the principles and values that you look to for guidance as you face life's moral challenges and ethical dilemmas. Next to each principle or value, list its source.

IV

MONEY & WORK

To learn the value of money, it is not necessary to know the nice things it can get for you[;] you have to have experienced the trouble of getting it.

~ PHILLIPE HÉRIAT (1946)

Mama's paternal aunt, Lela, comes to mind when I think about the relationship between money and work. In full rural, Black, Southern dialect, local elders pronounced "Lela" as *Leller*. As a child, my unrefined ears heard something different even still. I referred to her as my *Aunt Letter*.

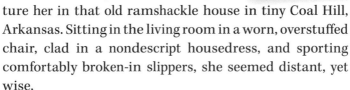

Aunt Lela lived into her nineties, and savored every moment. I still picture her in that old ramshackle house in tiny Coal Hill, Arkansas. Sitting in the living room in a worn, overstuffed chair, clad in a nondescript housedress, and sporting comfortably broken-in slippers, she seemed distant, yet wise.

Aunt Lela shared her house with her sister and diametrical opposite, Erma. Aunt Erma was rail-thin, taciturn, and possessed of a ghost-like knack for receding comfortably into the background. She neither made a fuss nor encouraged a fuss to be made over her. By contrast, Aunt Lela, rotund and talkative, unabashedly craved center stage. She made her presence known, and delighted in the attention she garnered. She relished life and its simple pleasures.

Her front door ajar on an oppressively hot summer day, Aunt Lela retreated to her time-honored routine, a seasonal ritual. Baseball provided the centerpiece. On our sporadic visits, Aunt Lela's gaze would invariably fix on her old, antenna-dependent television. The snowy, static-filled, black and white image of the boys of summer engaged in "America's pastime" lit up the room. Dipping dark, aromatic snuff from a small canister and sipping pale, cool beer from a silvery aluminum can, she radiated serenity.

Mama often repeated something that Aunt Lela used to tell my brother, David. Dave, eager to please and even more eager to earn extra cash, offered himself up as a lawn-mowing service. Aunt Lela seized upon Dave's offer, without first negotiating his fee. When Dave dutifully completed the task, a grateful Aunt Lela offered only this: "Thank you until you're better paid."

She needed someone to mow her overgrown yard. Dave made himself available. Often, Aunt Lela found herself short on cash. So, she offered her expression of appreciation and an implied promise of something more when she could afford it. Dave accepted that.

Aunt Lela believed that family should do things for one another simply because those things needed to be done. She made no apologies.

Mama used the story about Aunt Lela and Dave to illustrate that sometimes we should do things for reasons other than monetary rewards. Sometimes, a simple "thank you" works wonders: at least until you're better paid!

Mama's Pearls

 ~ Thank you 'til you're better paid.
 ~ Don't get your honey where you make your money.
 ~ Finance before romance.
 ~ You can't get blood out of a turnip.

MEDITATION

The Johnson kids made money by doing chores, mowing lawns, delivering newspapers, and making good grades in school. We worked hard for the little money we earned, and thus developed a healthy work ethic. We learned that money should not be an end unto itself. We discovered that money, while it can inspire and motivate, may also corrupt and debase. Ultimately, we choose which.

FIRST THINGS FIRST: Reflect on how the role of money in your life has evolved through the years. List your top five financial priorities. Is it possible to have "enough" money? If so, how much is "enough"?

V

TIME

Time makes more converts than reason.

~ THOMAS PAINE (1776)

Mama often reminded us that tomorrow may never come. Make the most of each minute of each hour of each day, she cautioned. Waste no time.

A parable set in the African wilderness illustrates the point. Every morning in Africa, a gazelle wakes up. It knows it must run faster than the fastest lion or it will be killed. Every morning in Africa, a lion wakes up. It knows it must run outrun the slowest gazelle or it will starve to death. It does not matter whether you are a gazelle or a lion: When the sun comes up, you had better be running.

Mama, through word and deed, stressed celebrating, honoring, and cherishing people while they live rather than waiting until the bell tolls to sing their praises. "Give me my flowers while I still live," became a prized piece of wisdom. Remarkably, Mama still gives folks flowers—always doing something simple and kind for someone else, expecting nothing in return.

Her senses of service, duty, and compassion trace back to her childhood. Mama, at age nine, became the mother of her household when her own mother died from complications of childbirth. Her five siblings, four younger sisters and an older brother, became her responsibility.

"Ma West," Mama's paternal grandmother, lived nearby. She provided the stability that the motherless family

21

so desperately needed. Mama's father, Alberry West, a World War I veteran and a family farmer, found his niche as a Missouri Pacific Railroad man. As a member of a Missouri Pacific Railroad section crew (also known as a "section gang"), he kept the tracks in good condition so that the trains could run safely and efficiently. Among other duties, he shifted the ballast and replaced ties, rails, spikes, and bolts when necessary.

"Mr. Alberry," as some affectionately called him, traveled frequently. His absences thrust Mama more deeply into the role of caretaker. She looked to Ma West for guidance.

Ma West gave lessons in living. "Grab a bucket and turn it upside down, child," she told Mama. "Then, just step right on up there. That way, you'll be able to reach the stove."

Mama, a willowy, callow, eager-to-please girl, took her "womanly duties" in stride. She did more than just cook. She tackled the cleaning, the laundry, and the ironing, too.

The ironing provided a severe test of endurance and diplomacy. Ma West insisted on modesty at all times and under all conditions. That meant dressing decorously—covering up—even in the scorching heat of the Southern summer. Ma West insisted that Mama wear a long skirt over her shorts, even while ironing. "Cover up, child. A proper girl doesn't show her legs," Ma West exhorted.

Sweat pouring down her brow, Mama alternated between the two irons heating on the coal-fired stove. Gripping one of the irons by its handle with a potholder to protect against the blistering heat, she dutifully starched and pressed freshly laundered clothes. As the iron in use cooled, she replaced it with its piping hot alternate. She repeated the laborious process until she completed all the day's ironing.

She complied with Ma West's strict dictates, at least while Ma West looked on. But as soon as Ma West set foot out of the house, Mama defiantly ripped off her overskirt, flung it asunder, and tended to her chores in the immodest comfort that only shorts afford. All the while, though, she surveyed the terrain with eagle-eyed vigilance. When she spotted Ma West returning home, she abandoned all sense of defiance, donning the cumbersome "cover-up" garment just as quickly as she had removed it.

And so it went—innocence lost. That baptism by fire shaped Mama's lifelong devotion to service—service to family; service to friends; service to community.

Mama provided a powerful role model, demonstrating that time *invested* in others often yields greater dividends than time *spent* on oneself. She taught us a timeless lesson: We honor ourselves and grow as individuals when, through service, we honor others.

Mama's Pearls

- A watched pot never boils.

- Better late than never.

- It's always darkest before the dawn.

- Tomorrow is not promised.

- The sun's gonna shine in my back door someday.

MEDITATION

Time is impatient. It waits for no one. Time is compassionate. It heals all wounds. Time is omniscient. It will tell. We can neither start nor stop the all-important force we call "time." At best, we can manage it judiciously, lending a sense of meaning and purpose to our lives. Make the most of each fleeting, precious moment. Always give it your best shot.

FIRST THINGS FIRST: List five ways that you can make optimal use of every moment of every day in the future. List five individuals to whom you owe a call, a letter, or an e-mail. Make a definite commitment to stop procrastinating and start communicating.

VI

SUCCESS & FAILURE

There are two ways of rising in the world, either by your own industry or by the folly of others.

~ La Bruyère (1668)

Mama and Dad made clear to me that I could do and be anything if I put my mind to it. "You, son, are as good as any," they consistently and emphatically reminded me. Given that unqualified support, I interpreted success as an obligation, not an option.

The Johnson family moved from Mineral Wells, Texas to Fort Smith, Arkansas in 1972. A thirteen-year-old at the time, this uprooting caused me great anxiety. Would I ever see my old friends in Texas again? Would I make friends in Fort Smith? Would I fit in with my new school peers? These questions, coupled with typical teenage angst, cast a pall over the beginning of my eighth grade year.

On a hot, sunny August day in 1972, Mama took me to audition for the band at my new school in Fort Smith, Kimmons Junior High. We arrived, and promptly met Richard Peer, the band director. Mama waited outside the band room as Mr. Peer led me to a practice room for the audition. Nervous yet confident, I plucked my dented, brass cornet from its tattered, caramel-colored case, grabbed my wrinkled sheet music, and pulled a black metal music stand in front of me. I gingerly placed the music on the stand, eagerly anticipating the chance to make a first and lasting impression. Mr. Peer instructed me to play a few basic musical scales, then gave me the green light to begin my prepared piece. I chose a "modern" piece, the Beatles' "Yesterday," for my debut. I completed it with relative ease, comfortable with my performance. Mr. Peer, reservedly impressed, remarked that the cornet/trumpet section had better watch out for me, the new kid in town.

Eventually, I rose to the "first trumpet" section, and ultimately, to "first chair." By year's end, my colleagues in the band elected me band president. Dad rewarded me with a new Bach Stradivarius silver trumpet, the gold standard among young trumpeters of the day.

Emboldened by my success in the band, I decided to run for student council president. I ran against Mark, a popular, likeable athlete and the odds-on favorite. My school, about ten percent Black, had never elected a Black student body president. Conventional wisdom discounted the prospect of my peers electing me, a *new* Black kid, as student body president. My campaign manager, Brian, assembled a diverse group of eighth graders to serve as my campaign committee. He hosted committee meetings at his house.

Brian seemed an unlikely ally and an even more unlikely campaign manager. By no means a stereotypically "popular" kid, Brian, a smart, chubby White kid with a military haircut, even carried a businessman's briefcase to school every day—a fashion *faux pas* by any standards. Despite our superficial differences, we genuinely admired one another. Somehow it all worked out. Perhaps our campaign slogan held the key: "Hannibal Johnson: The man with a plan!" Or perhaps one of our "cool" campaign signs swayed the voters: "Shaft was bad, Superfly was cool, but

Hannibal Johnson's the baddest dude that ever hit this school!" How could anyone resist?

My *modus operandi* began well before the campaign, and continued long after. My strategy boiled down to this: Be kind to everyone—treat everyone with respect. That meant, in a practical sense, smiling, speaking to people in the hallways, and developing a genuine interest in the affairs and well-being of others. I employed a strategy for successful living, not simply for a successful campaign. Ultimately, Brian believed in me and convinced a majority of my cohorts in the eighth grade to elect me president of the student council.

In life, only hollow success comes without kindness toward and respect for others. The best kind of success comes from being able to look in the mirror and recognize the reflection of a good person. That type of success serves as its own reward. I learned that from Mama.

Mama's Pearls

- Good, better, best; never let it rest; 'Til your good is better and your better is best.
- Nothing causes failure but a try.
- Don't build the roof before you've laid the foundation.
- Success doesn't come to you. You go to it.

MEDITATION

Those inevitable failures we all experience along the path to success need not deter us. Failure breeds opportunity, and the potential for even more success. Having someone believe in you unconditionally—and believing in yourself with like measure—cannot help but result in successful living.

FIRST THINGS FIRST: List ten pieces of advice you would give to someone who asked you how to live a successful life. On the same list, place a checkmark by the items of advice you follow in your life.

VII

RACE

To live anywhere in the world today and be against equality because of race or color, is like living in Alaska and being against snow.

~ WILLIAM FAULKNER (1965)

Mama and Dad insisted that my brothers, Magnus and Frank, and I memorize Edgar A. Guest's poem, *Equipment*. I still hear the echoes of my own nine-year-old-kid voice:

> So figure it out for yourself my lad,
> You've all that the greatest men have had;
> Two arms, two hands, two legs, two eyes,
> And a brain to use if you would be wise,
> With this equipment they all began.
> So start from the top and say, 'I can.'
> Look them over the wise and the great,
> They take their food from a common plate,
> And similar knives and forks they use,
> With similar laces they tie their shoes,
> The world considers them brave and smart,
> But you've all they had when they made their start.

You can triumph and come to skill,
You can be great if you only will.
You're well equipped for what fight you choose,
You have arms and legs and a brain to use,
And the man who has risen great deeds to do
Began his life with no more than you.
You are the handicap you must face,
You are the one who must choose your place,
You must say where you want to go,
How much you will study the truth to know,
God has equipped you for life, but he
Lets you decide what you want to be.
Courage must come from the soul within
The man must furnish the will to win.
So figure it out for yourself, my lad,
You were born with all that the great have had,
With your equipment they all began,
Get hold of yourself and say 'I can.'

Reprinted by Permission of the *Detroit Free Press*.

We practiced that poem until we could recite it with all the gusto we could muster. "Equipment," still hangs in my brother Frank's old room in my parents' home, decades after we memorized it. That jewel of a poem stood the test of time because it speaks to self-esteem and empowerment, the foundational armor we all need as we journey through life.

On those days when life seems particularly burdensome, I can recall "Equipment" for an infusion of confidence, courage and strength. It gives me an "attitude adjustment" when I need one. First learning the poem's ennobling words, then internalizing them, prepared me for a world that, from my parents' perspective, sometimes conveyed a contrary message.

Mama and Dad grew up Black in rural, segregated Arkansas. They knew from experience that race mattered.

As a result of this historical trauma, building their children's self-esteem early and reinforcing it often became a priority for them. They insisted that, despite the limitations others may try to impose, we could do whatever we dreamt of, and that we could do it as well as anybody. We took them at their word.

Mama's Pearls

~ *It takes many colors to make a rainbow.*

~ *The only race that matters is the human race.*

~ *Green is the only color that really matters.*

~ *The blacker the berry, the sweeter the juice.*

~ *Every dog has its day.*

MEDITATION

Race matters—less so than in the past—but it still matters. Fortunately, I grew up embracing the egalitarian notion of an indivisible humanity. We learned to respect others as we respected ourselves.

With Dr. Martin Luther, King, Jr. as my preeminent role model, I focused my attention on that which comes through refinement, "the content of [my] character," rather than on that which comes through birthright, the "color of [my] skin." I discovered that sometimes I would have to be better—more qualified, better prepared—than some of my counterparts to make up for the bias I faced. While I experienced no shortage of disappointments borne of race, I see progress. That progress gives us all reason for hope.

FIRST THINGS FIRST: List five things that you commit to do in an effort to improve race relations and intercultural understanding in your community. For each item listed, note a timeline and the resources/assistance you will need in order to be successful.

VIII

RELIGION

There is one spectacle grander than the sea, that is the sky;
there is one spectacle grander than the sky, that is the interior
of the soul.

~ VICTOR HUGO (1862)

Religion played a pivotal role in shaping my sense of self-esteem. It provided a moral and spiritual foundation upon which to build a productive, meaningful life. Because of Mama, a devout Christian, I attended church, well, "regularly": Sunday school, Sunday morning worship services, Sunday evening worship services, Wednesday night Bible study, summer vacation Bible school, periodic evangelistic revivals, and on and on and on.

If my church had maintained a choir, I would have joined, even in spite of my inability to carry a tune—*any tune.* The church I attended favored congregational singing of standards like *By and By, I'll Fly Away,* and *Amazing Grace* without instrumental accompaniment. So, I sang along with everyone else, off key, but on message.

I did more than merely pass time at the various church services and events. I became an integral part of a new "spiritual family," and evolved into a child of the church.

I honed my communication skills and poise at church. The church I attended as a teenager, a small, whitewashed stone structure at the corner of 9th & "S" Streets in Fort Smith, Arkansas, rarely attracted more that 100 worshippers. Because of its modest membership, everyone mattered at 9th & "S." The adults among the close-knit, working class congregants created abundant leadership opportunities for aspiring, energetic youth. I took full advantage. I burnished my speaking talents and boosted my confidence by reading the pre-sermon scripture, making door-to-door evangelistic appeals, and serving in the weekly communion and offering rituals.

I learned to pray. The initial focus centered on the mechanics of prayer. But I soon came to appreciate its real essence: reflection and gratitude.

I learned the virtues of charity and service by praying for the sick and the "'flicted" *(i.e.,* afflicted), visiting the sick and the shut-in, and tending the church grounds for no other reason than these things needed to be done. The people from whom I learned—fundamentally good people, plain folks making the best of what they had—provided a positive spiritual, educational, and social experience all rolled into one. I thrived in the midst of the nurturing cocoon they spun.

Mama never forced me to attend or to participate in the various services or activities. But I soon developed a strong internal impulse that compelled that result. Exposure to religion taught me virtues like honesty, integrity, compassion, charity, humility, and discipline. It helped me become a whole person.

Mama believed that all children should be afforded the opportunity to experience a spiritual journey. Amen to that!

Mama's Pearls

- The most important prayer in the world is just two little words: "Thank you!"

- Pray for a faith that will not shrink in the waters of affliction.

- An idle mind is the devil's workshop.

- God don't like ugly.

- Give the devil his due.

MEDITATION

Religion at its best gives a child a wonderful sense of grounding. The routine and ritual of religion help to foster discipline. A spiritual basis encourages reflection and engenders hope. A spiritual connection adds meaning to life, and helps form the foundation for whom and what we ultimately become.

FIRST THINGS FIRST: List five aspects of your life that have been deeply impacted by your religious or spiritual background. Note how religion or spirituality impacted those facets of your life. List some of the individuals who have been instrumental in your religious or spiritual growth.

IX

LOVE

Love is Nature's second sun.

~ George Chapman (c. 1599)

For many of us, that nearly indefinable word, "love," is inextricably intertwined with the word "mother." For me, an additional, albeit unlikely, two words tie "love" and "mother" together: "applesauce cake."

This unlikely association—this seeming *non sequitur*—may be less bizarre than it seems at first blush. As a child, Mama's deliciously moist applesauce cake ranked at the top of my food chain. Mama knew that, and made the delectable, sweet-but-not-too-sweet, treasure especially for me—at least I thought so at the time.

Her recipe called for a relative few simple ingredients: two cups of sugar, two eggs, one-half cup of shortening, one cup of chopped walnuts, one cup of raisins, two and one-half cups of flour, one teaspoon of soda, one teaspoon of baking powder, one teaspoon of cloves, one teaspoon of cinnamon, two cups of applesauce, and one teaspoon of vanilla. Those ingredients, infused with just a pinch of love and baked at 350 degrees until done, combined to create Mama's culinary masterpiece.

That cake, that flavorful comfort food, made me feel both special and loved. Even as a child, I could appreciate the time and care that went into baking that deliciously plain, but indescribably tasty, dessert.

Mama's savory applesauce cake came to symbolize love in action. She seldom verbalized that love. Instead, her actions spoke volumes. The message was unmistakable. Love had everything to do with it.

Mama's Pearls

~ You never miss the water 'til the well runs dry.

~ The only way to have peace in a relationship is to know how to butter your own bread.

~ Love whom you will, marry whom you must, but in God only put your trust.

MEDITATION

We know it when we see it, right? For many, "love" defies words. In the end, our actions tell the true story. Sometimes our greatest lessons in love come not from what we say, but rather from the signals we give. Love often speaks sign language.

FIRST THINGS FIRST: Define "love" in five words or fewer. List examples from your own life experience of love in action.

X

RESPECT

Without feelings of respect, what is there to distinguish men from beasts?

~ CONFUCIUS, *Analects* (6TH C. BC)

Mama and Dad taught us that respect for oneself and respect for others go hand in hand. They always carried themselves with dignity and honor. That message took a firm hold on all of us, but most assuredly on my sister, Brenda. Indeed, Brenda has been known to exclaim: *"I expect to be treated as no less than a queen!"*

What if we all regarded ourselves and others as "royalty" of sorts—royalty stripped of its tedious bow and curtsey formality, but still imbued with its sense of the regal, noble, dignified, and magnanimous? What if we treated one another as no less than kings and queens, each entitled to respect and duty-bound to give it in return?

During the heyday of Jim Crow, African-Americans devised clever schemes to maintain their dignity and garner respect. One such artifice centered on the naming of children. Not at all uncommon among generations of African-Americans are regal and honorific names like "Queen Esther," "Countess," "Lady," "Precious," "Prince," "Princess," and "Major." The mere utterance of such names connotes respect. Despite the injustices and slights the bearers of these monikers faced, they took no small satisfaction in the modicum of respect their names accorded them.

Getting beyond shallow, superficial notions of respect

requires more than contrivance or manipulation. It requires mutuality. Throughout the years, Mama has remained particularly adept at fostering a sense of community, no matter what the circumstances. Her secret is no secret at all: she consistently treats others with respect. She sees the best in others, even if prescription lenses sometimes become necessary. As family matriarch, "church lady," and neighbor, she is loved in large part because of her extraordinary knack for finding beauty in all others. Ultimately, that is what respect is all about.

Mama's Pearls

- You have to give respect to get it.

- I'd rather drink muddy water and sleep in a hollow log than to be mistreated like a low-down dirty dog.

- If you don't respect yourself, how can you expect other people to respect you?

MEDITATION

When it comes to respect, one gets as good as one gives. When we treat others with compassion and kindness, we bask in the afterglow. Like mirrors, our good deeds reflect back on us.

FIRST THINGS FIRST: Consider how we demonstrate respect for ourselves and others. List and prioritize five principal ways we demonstrate self-respect and five principal ways we show respect for others.

XI

EDUCATION

Education makes a people easy to lead, but difficult to drive; easy to govern, but impossible to enslave.

~ LORD BROUGHHAM
(House of Commons speech,
January 29, 1828)

My name has everything to do with education—and history. "Hannibal" marked me for life as unique, and spurred a lifelong intellectual curiosity.

Dad, a former teacher, vetoed Mama's proposed name for her sixth and final child. The two possibilities, worlds apart, revealed a deep fissure in patriarchal and matriarchal worldview.

Dad, his militant spirit never lurking far beneath the surface, insisted on a name resurrected from the annals of African history. Mama, by contrast, chose a pleasant, sweet sounding name without reference to its historical significance. Dad prevailed. On January 27, 1959, "Hannibal" conquered "Patrick."

I am certain that the triumph of "Hannibal" influenced my present passion for education. I knew at an early age that my name carried with it a special obligation to excel. Somehow, Mama and Dad instilled in me a sense of the great Carthaginian general's genius, and at every turn reminded me of my own capacity for similar brilliance.

Dad read voraciously from a veritable treasure trove of books, some housed at home and some in his "branch library" in our old house in Coal Hill, Arkansas. These works fell principally into two categories: those that extolled the historical achievements and accomplishments of Africans and African-Americans and those that decried the historical maltreatment of African-Americans.

The titles spoke volumes: *The Mis-education of the Negro; Soul on Ice; The Fire Next Time; The Autobiography of Malcolm X; The Souls of Black Folks; A Pictorial History of the Negro in America;* and *Black Like Me,* just to name a few. In the living room, Dad kept a much-used set of *Funk and Wagnalls* encyclopedias, together with select "Negro" history reference books, in a small, wooden bookcase with glass sliding doors. He placed a premium on knowledge and access to it.

His books, an impressive collection indeed, told only part of the story. As part of my basic training for the skirmishes to come, Dad talked openly and regularly about the formidable barriers Black people faced—about bias, bigotry, and racism—and about succeeding against the odds.

He and Mama always made clear that education, more than any other single thing, held the key to a better life. They expected superior academic performance. They demanded excellence. They offered abundant praise for achievement. "Education," they said, "is the one thing that no one can ever take away from you." Now I understand.

Mama's Pearls

- *Too soon we get old; too late we get smart.*
- *A long journey starts with one step.*
- *Experience is the best teacher.*
- *An empty wagon makes the loudest noise.*
- *Things ain't always what they seem.*

MEDITATION

Education is the great equalizer, the great leveler. We grow as individuals only to the extent that we open ourselves to new information, new knowledge, and new consciousness. Education serves as our gateway to limitless possibilities.

FIRST THINGS FIRST: Imagine that a mad scientist has created a pill that, when ingested, permanently freezes one's educational attainment at the sixth-grade level. The scientist presents you with an intriguing offer: If you ingest one of his pills, you will be paid $10 million dollars. Would you accept the alchemist's offer? List five reasons for your decision.

XII

INTEGRITY

Actions speak louder than words, but not as often.

~ 1966 FARMERS' ALMANAC

Mama and Dad seldom verbalized their emotions. Instead, they showed them in the most basic of ways: providing food, shelter, clothing; giving unending encouragement and support; and nurturing our intellectual growth and development. Their deeds spoke for themselves.

Edgar A. Guest summed up their unarticulated philosophy quite well in a poem called *Sermons We See*:

> I'd rather see a sermon than to hear one any day.
>
> I'd rather one should walk with me than merely show the way.
>
> The eye's a better pupil and more willing than the ear;
>
> Fine counsel is confusing, but example's always clear;
>
> And the best of all the preachers are the men who live their creeds,
>
> For to see the good in action is what everybody needs.
>
> I can soon learn how to do it if you'll let me see it done.

I can watch your hands in action, but your tongue
    too fast may run.

And the lectures you deliver may be very wise and
    true;

But I'd rather get my lessons by observing what
    you do.

For I may misunderstand you and the high advice
    you give.

But there's no misunderstanding how you act and
    how you live.

> Reprinted by Permission of the *Detroit Free Press*.

The sermons we see matter most—the setting of examples, the role modeling, the "doing," not the "saying."
Those sermons shape us as individuals. Mama and Dad
taught us to lead by example; to look around, see what
needs to be done, and do it; to back up the talk with the
walk. We each possess the capacity to use our own unique
gifts to inspire others to positive action.

Mama's Pearls

- A bird flies high, but it has to come down to drink.

- When nobody around you seems to measure up, it's time to check your yardstick.

- A gossip is a person who can give you all the details without knowing any of the facts.

- That's like the pot calling the kettle black.

- If it looks like a duck and walks like a duck and quacks like a duck, it ain't no chicken!

MEDITATION

When we align our behaviors with our professed principles and beliefs, we lead lives of integrity. This seemingly simple formulation belies the difficulty of synchronizing beliefs and behaviors. Leading a life of integrity requires continuous "self work." Imperfect though we may be, consciousness of our internal struggles and a lifelong commitment to find balance in our lives makes for better people, better communities, and a better world.

FIRST THINGS FIRST: What particular characteristics and behaviors come to mind when you hear the word "integrity?" List and prioritize the top ten items, then rate yourself either positive (+), neutral (0), or negative (-) on each.

XIII

CITIZENSHIP

In America there must be only citizens, not divided by grade, first and second, but citizens, east, west, north, and south.

~ JOHN F. KENNEDY
(campaign address,
October 12, 1960)

Less than fifty percent of Americans eighteen and older vote, even in high-profile, hotly contested Congressional and Presidential elections. How can so many citizens abdicate such a fundamental civic responsibility as suffrage—the franchise—so routinely and so blithely?

I vote. I always vote. For me, it is obligatory—a solemn responsibility; a patriotic duty.

Growing up, I watched Mama and Dad faithfully make their way to the polls for each and every election, rain or shine. They never debated whether to vote in this election or that. It made no difference to them if the ballot contained justice of the peace candidates, gubernatorial hopefuls, or presidential aspirants. They simply did it.

I surmised that there must be something behind their commitment to the democratic ritual of voting. As I grew older, I began to appreciate the fact that for them, the act itself symbolized a hard-fought victory in an ongoing civil rights struggle.

That struggle for respect and equality held center stage for them, most particularly, for Dad. A World War II veteran, Dad ruefully recalled the days when, as a Black man in

France, he finally felt like a first-class citizen; when America, even for Black veterans, seemed strangely foreign. As the painful reality of discrimination and denial ebbed, his desire to take advantage of each and every American right and privilege intensified. Voting became chief among them.

Mama and Dad knew what it meant to be disenfranchised—to be disallowed a voice in government. By their actions, they made clear: "Never again!"

Children learn by example. Mama and Dad served as fine examples of what it means to be a "good American." Political and civic participation, I learned, form integral parts of the definition.

I fondly recall the presidential election of 1968. That year, Dad took me to see presidential candidate Hubert Horatio Humphrey, Jr. in Dallas, Texas. We lived in Mineral Wells, Texas at the time, a small town only a couple of hours from Dallas.

That year felt like Armageddon. The Vietnam War raged. The body count mounted. Antiwar protests flared. Demonstrators burned draft cards. Assassins James Earl Ray and Sirhan Sirhan felled Dr. Martin Luther King, Jr. and Robert F. Kennedy, respectively. Riots erupted. President Lyndon Baines Johnson stunned the nation with his decision to forego another run for the presidency. The Democratic National Convention descended into chaos as antiwar protesters Abbey Hoffman, Bobby Seale, Tom Hayden, and Jerry Rubin stole the show in Chicago.

During the fall of 1968, my fifth grade class at Sam Houston Elementary School discussed the presidential campaign and the election intensely. Our election coverage culminated in a mock vote. The opportunity to see my candidate in the flesh prior to our class election ratcheted up my excitement level several notches. It proved an unforgettable civics lesson for a ten-year-old, and, equally important, a classic father/son moment.

For the record, in Mrs. Smith's fifth grade class at Sam Houston Elementary School, Democratic candidate Hubert Horatio Humphrey, Jr. and his opponent, Republican candidate Richard Milhous Nixon, ran neck-and-neck, much as they did with the electorate. The Independent candidate, segregationist George Wallace, came in a distant third. We all know how things turned out in the real world: Richard M. Nixon became America's thirty-seventh President.

Mama's Pearls

↗ No man, without his consent, is another man's slave.

↗ Many patches make up the American quilt.

↗ Ain't gonna let nobody turn me around.

MEDITATION

The art of citizenship requires being informed about, engaged in, and committed to one's community. Good citizens are accountable to their communities, and they hold their communities accountable to the highest ideals and standards.

FIRST THINGS FIRST: Name five individuals whom you consider to be "solid citizens." List the specific personal characteristics that you considered in making your selections.

XIV

PERSEVERANCE

Many strokes overthrow the tallest oaks.

~ JOHN LYLY
Euphues: The Anatomy of Wit (1579)

The folksy synonym for perseverance, "stick-to-itiveness," captures
the grit and determination that the
concept presupposes. Some people
manage to navigate through all man-
ner of trials, great and small, day in,
day out. They refuse to allow others
to thwart their objectives or scuttle
their plans. They find nothing so high
that they cannot get over it; nothing
so low that they cannot get under it;
nothing so wide that they cannot get around it. Perse-
verance—part confidence, part indomitability—defines
these individuals. Mama and Dad are among them.

My parents persevered through
the harsh economic conditions of
the Great Depression—the abject
poverty; the human suffering; the
crushing despair. They bore up under the social indignities of the Jim
Crow era—the rigid segregation; the
oppressive violence; the wholesale
political disenfranchisement. They
endured levels of pain and hardship
that should be heaped upon no living soul.

57

Amidst the stifling and oppressive poverty and racism, the artificially limited possibilities and the prematurely dashed dreams, they and many like them managed not just to survive, but to thrive. They constructed virtuous lives filled with profound meaning. How did they pull off such a remarkable feat? They summoned up from deep within themselves an ironclad will to persist through adversity. They focused their energies on what they had rather than on what they lacked. They conjured up a vision of the future that represented an improvement over the past and the present. They persevered.

That perseverance, that "stick-to-itiveness," that tenacious, "can do" attitude, proved infectious. Blessed with fewer obstacles and greater resources, I nonetheless find myself just as determined, just as dogged, just as dedicated. Perhaps the full story lies in the genes.

Mama's Pearls

- Give in, give out—but never give up.
- A steady drop makes a hole in a rock.
- Life is like a see-saw. It has its ups and downs.
- Fake it 'til you make it.
- My get-up-and-go done got up and went.

MEDITATION

More often than not, the seemingly unbearable can indeed be borne. People, all of us, possess the capacity not just to endure, but to overcome. Ultimately, the question becomes whether the challenge or burden presented is in fact *worth* bearing.

FIRST THINGS FIRST: Think of three situations in which you have had to persevere to reach your goal(s). List them, together with the resources and support that enabled you to be successful.

XV

HONESTY

God looks at the clean hands, not the full ones.

~ PUBLILIUS SYRUS
Moral Sayings (1ST C. BC),
715, tr. Darius Lyman

When I think of honesty, the first thing that comes to mind is *the look*. Remember *the look*—that unmistakable look some parents give that focuses like a laser on its target, freezes him in his tracks, and evokes that quizzical "What did I do?" countenance? Lying—something I never learned to do well—earned me *the look* on one particularly memorable occasion.

On the day in question, Mama agreed to baby-sit for a neighbor's daughter, Susan. Friends and frequent playmates, Susan and I, both around six years old, knew one another well. Something led to a dispute between us, something no doubt insignificant. We argued. We tussled. I slapped her (a fact about which I am, of course, less than proud). Fearing the wrath of Mama, I fled down the street and hid. Six-year-olds, despite extensive hide-and-go-seek training with their peers, tend not to fare well when the seeker is

an adult. Mama quickly and almost effortlessly tracked me down. I nervously feigned innocence.

My pretenses notwithstanding, I got *the look*. I knew that my time of reckoning had come. Mama marched me back home, scolding me as we went. Though the incident itself merited punishment of some sort, the lying, she said, magnified its seriousness tenfold.

Mama administered what seemed to be a merciless spanking that day—one of the few that I ever received. I recovered. I reflected. I reformed. I learned a little something about honesty that day.

Mama's Pearls

~ Eventually, the chickens will come home to roost.

~ Fool me once, shame on you. Fool me twice, shame on me.

~ Let your conscience be your guide.

MEDITATION

In the final analysis, honesty really is the best policy. Deception, even when successful in the short term, corrupts. Truth, though at times unpleasant and unwelcome, cannot be ignored without negative consequences.

FIRST THINGS FIRST: Think of an occasion on which you told a falsehood that entailed negative consequences. List the things you learned from the incident and describe your present-day views on truth-telling.

XVI

HUMILITY

Humility neither falls far, nor heavily.

PUBLILIUS SYRUS
Moral Sayings (1ST C. BC)
334, TR. Darius Lyman

My parents grew up poor and Black in rural Arkansas, a state now fondly dubbed "The Natural State." That nickname derives from Arkansas' unspoiled natural assets: scenic landscapes, ample wildlife, and abundant bodies of water. For Mama and Dad, humility came as naturally as the rustic, pastoral beauty that earned the state its moniker.

Rural roots anchored Mama and Dad in the virtue of service. They embraced servanthood as roundly as they eschewed servility. Like family, the rural Black folks in Arkansas helped one another when the need arose. Working with and for others was simply the right thing to do. The lessons these simple country folk learned growing up shaped their lives, and the lives of their children.

The example of service Mama and Dad set—service to family, service to faith, and service to community—inspired my own sense of obligation to make a difference. They modeled service and, in the process, practiced inspired leadership. I bore witness, not just as son, but as acolyte, pupil, and protégé.

Mama worked in the church, a labor of love. Dad toiled in the civil rights movement and in grassroots community organizations. He served less out of love and more out of conviction to cause, tinged with a hint of urgency. Taken together, their efforts instilled in me a sense that people everywhere are intertwined, interconnected, and

interdependent. Our interconnectedness—the mutuality and reciprocity inherent in our existence—should keep us all humble.

Some mistake humility for weakness or lack of ambition, seeing life only through the prism of self-interest. But the singular pursuit of self-interest restricts one's ability to see clearly. In humility lies perfect vision: the ability to see the universe without oneself at its center.

Mama's Pearls

~ Every tub must sit on its own bottom.

~ You'd better come down off your high horse.

~ There is some good in the worst of us and some bad in the best of us. So, it behooves all of us not to talk about the rest of us.

~ You've got to crawl before you walk.

~ You'd have thought that he parted the Red Sea!

MEDITATION

When we recognize that we are not the center of the universe, we free ourselves to serve others. In serving others lies true fulfillment. We grow as we serve.

First Things First: List three prominent people whom you would describe as humble. Beside each name, list several characteristics that influenced your decision to include that individual.

XVII

GRACE

Without grace[,] beauty is an unbaited hook.

~ French proverb

Difficult to define and even more troublesome to quantify, grace is a subtle quality. It adorns and embellishes. It nuances the things we do. That sense of grace manifests itself in a variety of ways, but perhaps none as palpable as in Mama's cooking.

We rarely dined out or partook of fast food. Mama cooked almost every day. In fact, I figure that I consumed more than 5,000 home-cooked dinners during my formative years, each infused with that special something.

Imagine a combination of down-home Southern cuisine and good old soul food: skillet-fried cornbread, baked cornbread, and "scratch" dinner rolls; collard greens, mustard greens, polk salad, cabbage, homegrown tomatoes, candied yams, black-eyed peas, corn-on-the-cob, pinto beans, boiled spinach, macaroni & cheese, and fried okra; fried chicken, baked ham, pot roast, pork chops, meatloaf, and ox tails; sweet potato pie, pecan pie, bread pudding, peach cobbler, and homemade ice cream. A pinch of grace flavored every dish.

A hint of Mama's grace touched other aspects as well. Wherever we lived, Mama always planted a lush, tidy flower bed bursting with color. A bouquet of brightly-colored, eye-catching zinnias formed the centerpiece. Clumps of white and rose-colored azaleas adorned the perimeter. Interspersed throughout the remaining space were yellow gladiolas, lavender morning glories, and luminous green elephant's-ears.

In addition to the flower bed, Mama often tended a small, backyard garden. Perennial favorites like crimson-colored tomatoes, yellow and green peppers, and deep green collards typically dominated the plot. These scrumptious, organic vegetables put their store-bought kin to shame.

Flower beds and gardens: These are grace notes. And that is what Mama does best. She brings that sense of grace—that special flair—to the things she does. Kindness, thoughtfulness, and appropriateness come together in ways that uplift the spirit.

I recall as a college student at the University of Arkansas, then as a law student at Harvard, receiving "thinking of you" cards and short handwritten notes intermittently. Invariably, the cards and notes enshrouded a twenty dollar bill (or, on special occasions, perhaps a fifty). That extra cash made a difference in my world. I understood and appreciated the sacrifice that it symbolized. That made a world of difference. We were by no means rich. Then again, perhaps we were richer than I realized.

Mama's younger sister, Doris, exhibits the same knack for felicitousness—the same salt-of-the-earth tendencies. Whether uttering a kind word to a stranger or checking in on an elderly neighbor, Aunt Doris goes the extra mile. She prides herself on doing just the right thing at just the right time.

For as long as I can recall, Aunt Doris' correspondence to me—notes, cards, telephone calls—has begun: "To my sweet, intelligent, handsome nephew" or "How's my sweet, intelligent, handsome nephew?" A recent belated birthday card proved no exception. The card's cover art, a colorful bouquet of flowers, accompanies its inscription, direct from the factory, but meticulously chosen by Aunt Doris: "Belated Birthday Wishes For Someone Very Special." Inside, she added: "Someone very kind; someone very intelligent; someone very full of wisdom, knowledge, and understanding; someone very handsome. All of these things make you someone *very special.*"

How do I react to such flattery? While I can only hope to live up to all that, I am nonetheless honored to know that someone sees me in that light—sees me moving in the right direction. Invariably, I smile. I feel special. My spirit soars. It seems unfailingly to be just the right thing at just the right time.

That is the point about grace. Small, seemingly simple gestures can transform—at least for a moment—the lives of others in ways we may never know.

> ## Mama's Pearls
> ❧ *When in doubt, don't.*
>
> ❧ *Walk circumspect.*
>
> ❧ *You can do well by doing good.*

MEDITATION

A lady, upon hearing the late, great gospel singer Mahalia Jackson perform, remarked that she had never heard anyone add so many "flowers and feathers" to a song. That is grace: the flowers and feathers that we add to the things we do.

FIRST THINGS FIRST: List three prominent people whom you would describe as possessing grace. Beside each name, list several characteristics that influenced your decision to include that individual.

XVIII

COMPASSION

The comforter's head never aches.

~ ITALIC PROVERB

It started as a dull, lingering sensation in the lower right abdominal area. I was fifteen, and in the ninth grade at Kimmons Junior High School in Fort Smith, Arkansas. At first, I ignored it. Having just won the local Optimist Oratorical Contest, I had set my sights on the state competition. And then there were my band obligations, my responsibilities as student council president, and the day-to-day rigors of academics. Stubbornly, I conceded nothing. I could not possibly allow a little twitch in the side to disrupt my neatly ordered priorities. Or so I thought.

Weeks later, the dullness sharpened; the sensation crescendoed into out-and-out pain. Finally, I shared my symptoms, as best I could, with Mama and Dad. They immediately took me to see our family physician, Dr. H.P. McDonald.

After the usual poking and probing, Dr. McDonald surmised that I might be experiencing appendicitis. Subsequent examinations and x-rays confirmed his suspicion. Diagnosed with acute appendicitis, surgery loomed inescapably on the horizon.

Within hours, the medical personnel scheduled the operation with a leading local surgeon. After admission to the hospital, I lost all sense of time. I remember waking up in a post-surgery funk. Sore, nauseous, and weak, I recall being buoyed by the presence of family and friends.

My failure to seek treatment at the onset of symptoms complicated the surgery. By the time of the surgery, my appendix had abscessed. Luckily, it did not burst. That could have been fatal.

All told, I remained hospitalized for three weeks. I lost twenty pounds, and grew exceedingly weak—so weak, in fact, that for several days after my release Mama had to physically support me as I walked. I looked like a zombie—gaunt, bug-eyed, and pale.

During the recuperative period, my friends and acquaintances from school called, dropped by, and asked other family members about my well-being. Teachers sent my assignments so that I could keep up with all my classes.

Once I returned to school, still emaciated, both schoolmates and teachers did what they could to get me through each day. Our student council sponsor, Mrs. Nancy Baker, even used her free time to take me to get milkshakes during lunch. I obviously needed "fattening up."

The compassion my family and friends showed during this difficult time more than made up for all the things I missed. Some lessons are better learned outside the classroom.

Mama's Pearls

⚬ God is love.

⚬ Blessed be the tie that binds.

⚬ What's good for the goose is good for the gander.

MEDITATION

Without action, compassion—knowledge of the plight of others, accompanied by the urge to assist—is but an empty vessel. When we know, care, *and act*, we elevate compassion beyond hollow sentimentality.

FIRST THINGS FIRST: List at least three occasions on which you have exhibited compassion and followed through with action. Try to recall the factors that motivated you on those occasions.

XIX

OPPORTUNITY

Chance favors the prepared mind.

~ LOUIS PASTEUR

My hometown, Fort Smith, Arkansas, boasts an increasingly diverse population, roughly 75% European-American, 9% African-American, 9% Hispanic American, 5% Asian-American, and 2% Native American. Part of the explanation for the rich diversity in this Western Arkansas border town of 80,000 lies in nearby Fort Chaffee.

Fort Chaffee, now a maneuver center for National Guard and U.S. Army Reserve soldiers, trains some 50,000 soldiers annually. Since its opening in 1941, Fort Chaffee has been one of America's key military installations. Thousands of military personnel began their careers there.

From 1943–1946, Fort Chaffee housed some 3,000 World War II German prisoners of war. Decades later, it served as a refugee processing and resettlement center. In 1975, the Fort Chaffee Refugee Processing Center served over 50,000 Vietnamese refugees who fled their country following the end of the Vietnam War. From 1980 – 1982, the Fort Chaffee Cuban Refugee Resettlement Center processed some 25,000 Cuban refuges from the so-called "Mariel Boatlift." Large numbers of both of these refugee populations remain in Fort Smith.

As a student at Fort Smith Northside High School ("NHS") in the mid-1970s, I witnessed the beginning of the incredible change in that community, heralded by the arrival of the Vietnamese refugees. The NHS band even ventured out to Fort Chaffee to entertain the throngs of newcomers. Eventually, sponsor families adopted the refugees and assisted with their integration into the community.

The immigrants began to settle in, gaining proficiency in English, finding homes, and seeking work. Dad, an employment counselor with the Arkansas Employment Security Division in Fort Smith at the time, became a key player in this massive cultural transition. His client demographics changed rapidly, as more and more Vietnamese entered the job market.

Sensitive to the prospect of discrimination, intentional or inadvertent, Dad took pains to be fair. He worked as hard for his Vietnamese clients as he did for everyone else—and perhaps harder. He successfully placed countless refugees.

To say that the new immigrants for whom Dad found employment were grateful would be a gross understatement. Indeed, to express thanks, they wrote "thank you" notes, called our house to express thanks and blessings, and even dropped by the house, frequently bearing gifts such as billfolds, clocks, and various other "whatnots."

Some of the families invited Mama and Dad to their homes for dinner.

"No, you don't understand," Dad would say, "this is my job; this is what I get paid to do." Thankful for the opportunity, the chance to earn a livelihood, these Vietnamese people—these new Americans—felt compelled to express their sentiments in ways that left no doubt about the breadth and depth of their gratitude.

Our opportunities are no more and no less than what we make of them. Fort Smith's immigrant Vietnamese population, now thriving by virtually any measure, attests to that.

Mama's Pearls

- Make hay while the sun shines.
- One man's junk is another man's treasure.
- If you lag, you'll lose.

MEDITATION

Opportunities abound. Some are readily apparent. Others come to us under the guise of some challenge or threat. No matter the particulars, however, it is incumbent upon us to be prepared when they arrive. If we are not, one thing is certain. Someone else will be.

FIRST THINGS FIRST: Recall and list an occasion on which you missed an opportunity. Describe the incident, and note what you might have done differently to seize the moment.

XX

HOPE

One can never consent to creep when one feels an impulse to soar.

~ Helen Keller

Sometimes in rickety wagons, other times in old flatbed trucks, the "Coloreds" in tiny Coal Hill, Arkansas made their way to the nearby "bottoms." They labored from sunup to sunset—a grueling, uninterrupted, monotonous dance on an earthen Southern stage. All the while, they held steadfast to hope; to the promise of brighter days ahead for them and theirs.

Dutifully and without complaint, they toiled in the wide expanse of a cotton field, realm of that great Southern monarch, King Cotton. They dressed in overalls on top of long-sleeved shirts. Straw hats adorned the men's heads. The women donned bonnets. Both men and women wore whatever shoes they had. Some of the field hands sported gloves with the fingers cut out so as not to impede the intricate work of picking cotton. Some sang, not on account of joy, but rather on account of boredom borne of routine and redundancy.

Mama, starting at age ten, accompanied her father to the cotton fields during the fall picking season. Her childhood curiosity dulled the sting of the experience, numbing her to the full brunt of its brutality. Nonetheless, she, even as a child, knew something of the harshness between the four corners of the field.

Farmers planted long rows of cotton in the spring for fall harvest. For what amounted to a mere pittance, workers chopped the cash crop in the oppressive Southern heat with hoes. "Backbreaking" scarcely begins to describe the physical ordeal, the drudgery, of picking cotton.

They picked the fluffy fiber manually. The routine wreaked havoc on ungloved hands. Exposed fingers bled from brushes with the waist-high cotton stalks whose blooms transformed into the rough, prickly bowls shrouding the precious commodity. Legs grew weary, limp from standing hours on end. Many a worker picked on bended knee.

Workers soon learned the rhythms of the fields they worked. In any given cotton field, the bowls opened at different times. After the first picking—the first pass at the field—workers completed a second picking, gathering whatever cotton remained in this final pass.

Uncle Bud ran the cotton field Mama sometimes worked. A sharecropper, Uncle Bud kept the books and paid workers for their day's work. He weighed croker sacks—burlap bags—full of cotton, then remitted payment: pennies on the pound. A couple of field hands then emptied the cotton-filled croker sacks into a wagon or truck. As a sharecropper, Uncle Bud fared little better than his field hands when it came to money. They all struggled to eek out an existence.

So much work; so little pay: Why did they do it? They did it because they had no choice. They needed money to make ends meet, so they did what they could. They knew that better days lay ahead for them and, if not for them, then for their children and their children's children. Hope got them through the day.

Mama's Pearls

- ➤ What you can conceive, you can achieve.

- ➤ Hitch your wagon to a star.

- ➤ Trouble don't last always.

- ➤ What you think about, you bring about.

MEDITATION

The absence of hope leaves a vacuum too often filled with desperation. Desperation fuels actions destructive of both self and others.

No matter how bleak and barren life's landscape may sometimes seem, we are neither the first nor the last to traverse its forbidding contours. To be sure, things could always be better. But it is equally true that things could always be worse. When we embrace a sense of hope, we are appropriately mindful of both of these complimentary propositions.

FIRST THINGS FIRST: Consider the social movements inspired by leaders like Mahatma Gandhi, Dr. Martin Luther King, Jr., and Nelson Mandela. What role did hope play in their personal lives and in the movements they led?

EPILOGUE

*E*ach of us is the product of a number of powerful influences. For many of us, the person whom we call "mama," "mother," "ma," "mom," "ma dear," or even "mommy dearest" looms large among those who shaped and molded our lives. These masons of the hearth gave us the building blocks with which to construct inspired, inspiring lives and legacies.

Ultimately, though, the course of a life turns on self-determination. We choose our individual paths. The choices we make and the consequences they yield hold enormous power over our destinies.

Many of us credit our mothers with instilling in us the core beliefs and values that facilitate good choices. After all, what good is self-determination without self-esteem— a mature understanding of oneself and one's relationship to the larger world? The universal, bedrock principles many mothers inculcate—honesty, compassion, perseverance, humility, respect, and integrity among them— form the compass that points us toward good choices and right paths.

Mama Used To Say explores some of the choices I made at various points along my own personal journey. More importantly, however, it examines the foundational underpinnings—the ethical moorings—of those choices. May the words, wit, and wisdom that have proven invaluable to me be equally beneficial to you.

ABOUT THE AUTHOR

Hannibal B. Johnson

Hannibal B. Johnson received his Juris Doctorate degree from Harvard Law School and his Bachelor of Arts degree from The University of Arkansas. He is an attorney, college professor, consultant, and author whose works include: *Black Wall Street—From Riot to Renaissance in Tulsa's Historic Greenwood District; Up From The Ashes—A Story About Community*; and *Acres of Aspiration—The All-Black Towns in Oklahoma.* Johnson, a frequent keynote speaker on topics ranging from diversity to leadership to non-profit governance, also works extensively with programs that foster positive youth development.